Depression On-the-Go:

An Interactive How-To Survival Guide for the Depressed and Those Who Love Them

By: Rena K. Seidler

Olives to those who stand beside me.

Dreams

Hold fast to dreams
For if dreams die
Life is a broken-winged bird
That cannot fly.
Hold fast to dreams
For when dreams go
Life is a barren field
Frozen with snow.

– Langston Hughes

Table of Contents

Prologue

Hello, my name is Rena and I'm Crazy, or rather, I am depressed. Yeah, it doesn't have quite the same ring to it as it does for Alcoholics. Alcoholics say there is a stigma against them, and I don't disagree. But what about the stigma against the mentally ill?

We don't have a six month chip. We don't have a sponsor. And we most certainly don't have the same socially acceptable support system. More importantly, we cannot simply avoid places that service our addiction, namely because our problem, depression, is not an addiction, it's an illness that is trapped with us at all times. The question is: how do you escape your own thoughts and feelings?

My heart hurts every day. Sometimes it's a twinge and sometimes it's an all-consuming fire. And that is the life of the chronically depressed. This book is for those of you who feel the same way, or for those who hope to better understand what depression is like. Because depression doesn't just hurt the ill, it hurts everyone that loves them as well. I do not have all the answers. I do not have a Ph.D. or an M.D (although if all of those letters are important to you, I do have two B.A.s (one in psychology) and a J.D.). I also have the past thirty years, and for well over half of those years I have lived battling various stages of depression. This book is not about studies or offering innumerable concrete facts; it is a book about the reality of depression. I want to try to help you. Please give me a chance.

And feel free to take a sneak peek at the end of this book. This is one time where the ending is not a spoiler. At the back, you will find some pages to help you on your way. Some are fun, some definitely are not. And some are there just in case they help, or maybe bring a smile to your face. Good luck.

CHAPTER 1

It's Not You, It's Me...and You, ...and..., Well, You Get the Idea

It's easy to say that depression is an ailment like any other medical condition. Of course, a broken arm is fixable with a cast, a skinned knee is cured with a bandage, and even cancer has the possibility of chemotherapy and/or radiation. Doctors can often fix the ailments that they can see. But, let's get something straight: no one can help cure your depression if you do not open up about your feelings and what is causing them.

All people experience sadness, and most experience at least mild depressive states at some point in their lives, perhaps caused by the death of a loved one, or the loss of a job. Sadness is not depression. And unlike a broken arm, the symptoms of depression may easily be hidden under a mask of sadness to those around you. You are not the only person to tell a friend that you have been diagnosed as depressed and hear in response, "Oh, I noticed you were sad."

More importantly, depression and other mental illnesses do not come with a compass that points straight north to the focus of the problem. Again: Julie fell off her bicycle, breaking her arm and skinning her knee; a malignant tumor grew in Michael's lung, causing his cancer diagnosis. But where do we begin with depression?

I spent one evening alone at my home. Just me, my dogs, a glass of wine, and the DVR. It had the makings of a perfect evening, until I was suddenly overwhelmed by a tidal wave of emotion-panic, anxiety, sorrow, and loneliness. I was overcome by a wave of depression. And unfortunately for all of us, the path to wellness is none to clear.

1. Nature versus Nurture

Good news, depression is caused one hundred percent by nature, so we can blame it on those good old genes passed down from mom and dad, and call it a day. Kidding! Actually, assuming we were raised by our parents, I guess we can still blame them with the nurture argument, too. That could certainly come in handy during an argument someday.

Seriously though, who knows which aspects of depression we are genetically predisposed to and which aspects we pick up along the life journey. Certainly, doctors do not seem to believe that nature or nurture, alone, determines who is susceptible to depression.

When you fill out that generic questionnaire every doctor's office has (you know the one) there is a reason it asks if any of your immediate family suffers or has suffered from depression at some time in their lives. I suspect my marking yes for my mom, dad, one grandma, two uncles, two cousins, and one brother is probably a bit of red flag for them. Or so I hope.

Yet even the most genetically perfect person is certainly susceptible to depression. How many perfectly happy people have still not fully recovered from 9/11 and Hurricane Katrina? Or what about my family, that learned the hard way about the meaning of a traumatic brain injury, when the nineteen-year-old baby of the family got drunk and drove his car into a tree? His best friend walked away from that same accident with a sore finger. My brother is in a wheelchair, with permanent severe memory and other brain issues. It has been nearly two years and my family still has not recovered. The point, of course, is that whether you are a genetic superstar or a physically, emotionally, verbally, or sexually abused individual from a broken family, anyone can suffer from depression. Depression does not discriminate.

2. The "Why" Factor

"When one door closes, another opens. But we often look so regretfully upon the closed door that we don't see the one that has opened for us." - **Helen Keller**

Regardless of why or how YOU came to join the depression 'family,' I know you have the desperate desire to point a finger at something or someone and say, "There! That is the cause of my depression." As you know, because you feel or have felt this way, or because you know someone who has, getting past the finger-pointing concept is so very hard. The truth is, you probably do not have enough fingers to point at the "reason," for your depression, because depression is not necessarily caused by any one moment in time.

> **FAMILY & FRIENDS**: I hope you pay close attention to this section because your loved one's depression is not your fault. So please, be supportive for them, and not harmful or destructive toward yourself.

o return to my own fifteen-year long battle with epression, I have spent a seemingly infinite amount f time trying to find the "Why" Factor of my own epression (ie. Why am I depressed?). I have had iree monumentally depressing occurrences in my 'e: a) my biological mom kicking me out of her ome when I was seventeen, 2) a dear friend's tragic eath when I was twenty-five, and 3) my brother's car accident when I was twenty-eight. The problem is, none of those can be the "Why" of my depression, because I was diagnosed depressed almost two-years before the first, ten-years before the second, and almost twelve-years before the third.

Alrighty then, how about...I was emotionally abused by my biological mom throughout my childhood, after my parent's got divorced in 1983, culminating with her kicking me out of her home without cause. Or, when they were young, my mom and dad were both so emotionally screwed up that they married so they would not have to be alone, and conceived yours truly, despite their apathy toward each other. Or better yet...well, you get the idea. Before long, we are blaming Eve for picking fruit from a tree.

For those of you with depression, I know you have played the "Why" game in your head a million times. For those of you who are trying to understand depression, welcome to our world. It is not logical. It is not helpful. And it is certainly not healthy. But the "Why"s won't go away just because you want them too.

Now's your chance. Feel free to write down some of your own "Why's." It will be our little secret, unless you decide to share it.

_____

_____

_____

_____

_____

_____

_____

_____

_____

_____

_____

_____

_____

_____

Unfortunately, some people never get past the finger pointing stage. Personally, I struggle with it, on some level, more days than not; but, my awareness of my unhelpful thinking helps me from being consumed by the "Why" Factor. For people who are caught in the "Why", it does not matter how old or young you are. It is never too late to work on getting better. It is also completely acceptable to slip up.

Depression is a deep black pit of pain and tears and terror ebbing and swelling inside your chest. You know it. I know it. For some, that struggle may be situational, and for some, that struggle may be forever. But what is important to remember is that ruminating on the "Why" Factor is not going to get you anywhere. At least not by itself.

The process of fighting depression, and it is a battle, is extremely different for each and every person. Most people will probably need to address their "Why" to some extent, if for no other reason than to say it aloud. I have found that acknowledging my own personal demons makes them a little less frightening. You can only learn from your past if you acknowledge it. But, remembering is not necessarily the same as conquering. It is always nice if you do succeed in vanquishing some demons, but even if you do not, good for you for taking the time to remember what has been, in an effort to change what will be.

It may be very difficult to look at your past. Abuse, war, death, pain- none are things that anyone wants to face a first time, let alone a second. And I certainly do not advocate that everyone should lie on a couch and describe every detail of their past. But some moments may be too big to ignore. Only so many elephants can fit in one room before it is so crowded you do not know right from left or up from down. Still, some people find it easier to continue on their life journey without looking back. And who am I to say that their way is wrong? On the other hand, I have never seen a healthy flower grow without acknowledging its roots.

3.   Sign Language

"I don't think we define our lives by our illness. We define ourselves by how we live."
- Larry Goldstein

Unfortunately, just because you recognize that you or someone near you is clearly off their emotional A-game, that does not mean you can wave a magic depression wand and tell if they are simply feeling 'blue,' or are in need of some serious help. Here's the thing: depression is scary. Depression is so overwhelming that it is hard to even put into words all of the pain and emotions swirling through your head. And it is even harder to step up and say, "I am depressed, please help me." With my family and close friends, it works best for me to say, "I'm not feeling so great," or even to simply text message them and ask them to call me when they can. These are cues that they recognize, meaning that I am in need of some help, or at the very least, some TLC.

Moreover, there are also ways for you, and your friends and family, to recognize depression. Below is a list of just a few common, non-verbal cues that depression might be brewing. Take a close look at this list for familiar feelings, and add others that you think may be important. The better you understand what you are fighting, the easier it is to beat.

a._____ isolating from others

b._____ difficulty concentrating and making decisions

c._____ insomnia

d._____ persistent feelings of sadness or anxiety

e._____ feelings of guilt or worthlessness

f._____ empty feelings

g._____ change in appetite

h._____ feelings of hopelessness/helplessness

i._____ thoughts of suicide

j._____ suicide attempts

k._____ ruminating on negative thoughts.

l._____ _____

m._____ _____

n._____ _____

o._____ _____

p._____ _____

The point is, regardless of what "symptoms," you may or may not see or feel, it is always acceptable to reach out. If you are in pain, call a friend, call a family member, or call a professional. Keep someone in your life who recognizes that you need help, because once you are in the midst of a depressive cycle, it may be very hard to directly ask for love and support. In the midst of a past depressive cycle, a friend recognized that I was having a difficult time and reminded me that he would always be my friend. Little words can have a huge impact, particularly for someone feeling isolated and depressed.

If you know someone in pain, offer a shoulder to cry on, or simply a night out to escape life's daily stressors, and if necessary, remind your friend or loved one that professional help is available. Strengthening your relationships when times are good makes overcoming difficult times that much easier. It can seem nearly impossible to take care of basic hygiene needs in the midst of depression, and having a well-developed network of loved ones is important to help you from slipping into an even deeper depressed state.

Reflection Section:_____

_____

_____

Author's Note: At the end of each chapter, you will find a "Reflection Section." No, it's not because I think I am so brilliant that you will want to bask in my greatness. It's because I find that where depression is concerned, sometimes answers lead to questions, and so on and so on. By writing them down, or simply taking a moment to consider something that sparked your interest, you may be closer to finding some of your own answers.

CHAPTER 2

Doctor Who?

"He's turned his life around. He used to be depressed and miserable. Now he's miserable and depressed." - **David Frost**

Do you have to see a professional of some sort to get past depression? Not to the best of my knowledge. You *can* also get over a broken arm without a professional, although I seriously doubt most people would want to. Of course, seeing a professional in the 'mental' world is a bit different.

First, many people worry about the possible taboo if they are "found out" to be in need of such help. Remember the to-do made over former First Lady Laura Bush's history of taking an antidepressant at some point in her life? Well, you are likely not that famous, so *un*fortunately for you, it is not all that likely anyone will ever find out or stigmatize you for it. Plus, (and maybe it's just me) out of my five best friends and myself, half of us have been to a mental health professional at some point in our lives, so seeking help does not make you that unique either. Sorry. The fact is, most people I know in both my personal and professional life are unaware of my psychiatric history, or at least they were until they picked up this book.

Seeking help for emotional matters is not shameful. If you, or someone you know, seems to be suffering from depression, be brave. Bravery does not mean standing stoically through the pain; it means getting help through a bad period in your life. Like most medical conditions, untreated depression can and may get worse over time. In a few, terrible instances, it can even be physically harmful or life threatening.

Seek help. You do not necessarily need

therapy, and you do not necessarily need a medical doctor, but that does not mean that one or both of them cannot help you get back to being 'you' in as short a time as possible.

1.   Dr. Shrink

"Psychiatry enables us to correct our faults by confessing our parents shortcomings."
- **Laurence J. Peter**

One professional option is a psychiatrist, also known as a licensed medical doctor who has graduated from medical school and is board certified to administer medicine. While your family doctor can prescribe psychiatric medication as well, a psychiatrist is specialized in working with mental illness. Most insurance companies seem comfortable with allowing some type of psychiatric care, and if your insurance allows you to see a psychiatrist over a family doctor, I highly recommend it.

There are a myriad of psychiatric medications out there, with side effects ranging from hallucinations to headaches, and nausea to seizures. Adding insult to injury, some of them are linked with an increase in suicidal thoughts and actions. This time I'm not kidding. Depression is a nasty illness, and many of the drugs used to fight it are very strong, and potentially very dangerous if you are not under proper medical care. Believe me, having your throat swell shut and breaking out in hives in a college freshman English class is so NOT cool. That is why it is unbelievably important to maintain regular appointments with your doctor, and keep him/her updated on any side effects.

Side Note: While we are talking medicine, this is NOT the way to attempt suicide. For most medicines, you need a ridiculous amount to be effective. On the other hand, you can easily end up in the emergency room having disgusting and painful treatments inflicted on you, and you have the possibility of causing yourself permanent physical or mental damage. Medicines can do a lot of good. And that is the only reason you should be using them.

2. Dr. Quack Quack

Another professional option is seeking out a psychologist's care. Psychologists can come with a wide variety of degrees including an M.A. or Ph.D., and can focus in a vast array of specialties that will be discussed later in this Chapter. Unlike psychiatrists, who focus in medical care and spend significantly less time in therapy, psychologists, also known as therapists or counselors, are not licensed to distribute medication. Instead, they spend time, typically in one-hour sessions, verbally addressing whatever issues you wish to discuss.

If this is your first time considering therapy, there are several things you should know. First, for the most part, it is confidential, and your psychologist will explain the confidentiality guidelines to you. Second, with a good psychologist, generally you are talking and they are listening—the point of therapy is not for the psychologist to solve your life problems, but for you to explore some of your personal issues yourself and perhaps pick up a coping skill or two. Third, insurance will often cover both psychologists and psychiatrists, so you do not necessarily need to choose one over the other. While my particular brand of depression does need medication to keep me stabilized, I greatly enjoy the many benefits I receive from my therapy sessions. Therapy gives you the opportunity to actually address your stressors, instead of simply medicating yourself into 'happiness.'

3. Don't Stop...Think About Tomorrow!

"Learn from yesterday, live for today,
hope for tomorrow."

- Albert Einstein

Umm...duh. When something works, you keep doing it. You absolutely should NOT stop therapy and/or medications the moment you feel better. In reality, steadily maintaining your medication and therapy schedule is much more difficult than it sounds, and this problem is very hard for family and friends to comprehend. Logic says I feel normal, ergo, I am normal. I know what it is like to want to feel 'normal,' but there is a reason you need that medication (and/or therapy), and you should only taper off of it under a doctor's careful supervision.

I am twenty-nine and I take more pills a day than my grandmother. And there is nothing normal about that. But because of those pills, I get to feel normal, act normal, sometimes even be normal. Without the pills, I bounce off walls (usually not literally), cry myself to sleep, and curl up in the fetal position on the couch.

Even worse, do NOT go off the medication because you think it is not working. Been there, done that. The problem may not even be the medicine, but instead your own ridiculous body. Apparently, on occasion bodies get spunky and need a change of flavor to keep them under control. So maybe you will need a different medicine, or maybe you will need a different dosage. But, that is a doctor decision, not a decision for you, especially not when you are hurting.

Reflection Section:_____

_____

_____

_____

_____

_____

_____

CHAPTER 3

Therapizing

"The psychoanalysts pick our dreams as if
they were our pockets."
- **Karl Kraus**

Yep, I totally made that word up. Yet nevertheless, I therapize each and every week, and many weeks I visit my Shrink too. Therapy is an amazing process. Or a horrific experience. Or somewhere in between. The problem with therapy is that the therapy you receive can only be as good as the therapist who gives it.

When I was sixteen, I went to an extremely unethical therapist. First, she had seen my biological mother years before, and should never have seen me since I was having some difficulties with my mom that I wanted to discuss during therapy. My mom kicked me out of her home for reasons that will never be clear to me, and I was not dealing with the situation well at all.

Second, that therapist broke my mom's confidence in a horrifying way and told me something I should never have been told. Something from my mom's past that had absolutely nothing to do with me or my mental health. Something that haunts me to do this day. Fortunately, that therapist has long since retired and cannot harm anyone else. That being said, if you feel that your therapist has acted unethically, you can, and should, report their actions to the American Psychological Association.

I share my story with you because choosing a therapist really is a huge decision. Ask a trusted doctor for a recommendation, or perhaps a friend you know who goes, or has gone, to therapy. My current therapist, whom I adore, was recommended by a friend. And there was no conflict there, since, fortunately, my friend and I have no issues that would conflict for the therapist.

1.Typo Therapists (Pretty Pun-ny, Right?)

There are many different types of therapists, from Freudian to Pavlovian. Kidding. Like I said, I am hardly the expert on psychological schools of thought. Still, there are things to know. For example, some therapists specialize in children, so if you know a hurting child, a child psychologist may have a much better chance of relating quickly and bonding successfully with the child. There's also couples therapists, music therapists, therapists that specialize in abuse, war veterans, and childhood trauma. Heck, a dear friend of mine focuses on men's issues. The question is: how do you know if you need a specialized therapist? And assuming you don't need a specialized therapist, who DO you need?

2. How to Choose

"I've had a perfectly wonderful evening.
But this wasn't it."
- **Groucho Marx**

For most people, jack-of-all-trade therapists will probably meet your needs. Certainly, my current therapist does a little bit of a lot of things, and she is amazing. General therapists are great for discussing current life issues: work, kids, significant others, money troubles, stress, normal life stuff that has brought you into the depressed state you are in. I do not mean to give the impression that past issues cannot and will not come up with a general psychologist, but rather that no particular issue is necessarily focused on throughout your relationship with him/her.

My therapist and I have recently discussed the idea of me seeing a second therapist. I'm really not that crazy, I swear! That being said, I do have some serious issues from a period of my life that I have had a great deal of difficulty getting over, and my therapist and I have talked about me seeing someone who specializes in that type of therapy. A therapist who I would only address childhood issues with, and not my current life. To be perfectly honest, I have not decided if that is for me. I don't know if I really need to open that can of worms. But if I do decide to, it is nice to know it is an option.

BEWARE! I do not know of a single insurance company that will pay for two therapists at once. Nonetheless, my point is simple: there is no right or wrong way to choose a therapist. Find someone you click with. If you do not feel like you can open up to them, find someone else. For you to get help you need to be with a counselor who you feel can help you. If you cannot be honest with your therapist, you will not succeed in fully working through your issue. If you do not fully work through your issues, you are increasing the likelihood that your depression will return.

And remember, just because a particular therapist meets your needs at one point in your life, does not mean they will necessarily meet your needs at a later point. There is no rule that prohibits you from choosing different counselors at different times. Certainly a couple's counselor will not be very helpful if you suddenly become depressed over work issues. More importantly, your personal issues may affect what type of therapist you are most comfortable with.

a. Male v Female

I know, this seems like a strange section to include. You may be thinking, "What possible difference could my therapist's sex make?" Obviously, sexual trauma, or another form of abuse, may lead you to being more comfortable with one sex or another. More than that, though, men and women have very different ways of communicating in the real world, and that same trend can follow in therapy.

I have certainly had direct therapists of both sexes, and open and honest therapists of both sexes. However, male therapists seem more direct and to the point, which at certain times in my life has been intimidating. On the other hand, female therapists generally seem more empathetic, which I truly enjoy, although I also find it is easier to change topics if I start to feel too pressured by a conversation. Keep this in mind when you choose your therapist. Find a therapist that has a personality to challenge yours, without overwhelming it.

3. Group Therapy

Another type of therapy, not as commonly known outside of inpatient services, is group therapy. Many people assume therapy groups are specialized: alcoholics, abuse victims, PTSD survivors. And while those groups certainly do exist, many cities also offer general therapy groups. These groups may be a little more difficult to find, but they are well worth the effort, particularly because many of them are completely free of charge.

If you are interested in looking into group therapy in your area, ask your family doctor, psychiatrist or psychologist for a recommendation. Churches also often offer therapy groups, both faith-based and open sessions. Your local community center or YMCA may also have therapy groups open to the public.

I have been to numerous group therapy sessions, and while it is more difficult for me, personally, to open up in a group, I find it hugely beneficial to hear others voice 'my' thoughts. It is one thing to be told you are not alone in the depths of depression, it is another thing completely to hear from someone else that they are experiencing feelings identical to your own.

Another beneficial aspect of group therapy is that you have an opportunity to meet people who are may be feeling some of the same social anxieties that you are feeling. Depression causes many people to isolate, and those who understand the feeling of isolation may be more receptive to engaging in a social activity with you. Use group therapy as a valuable opportunity to make new friends.

FAMILY & FRIENDS: For those who may be invited by your loved one to attend a group therapy session, it is entirely acceptable to go. Consider group therapy an opportunity to learn more about depression: how it feels and what it means.

Reflection Section:_____

_____

_____

_____

_____

_____

_____

_____

_____

_____

_____

_____

CHAPTER 4

If I had a Nickel for Everytime Someone Said, "You'll feel better soon," and Other Useless Nonsense

Family. Friends. Gotta love 'em. Yet I have never met a depressed person that didn't want to strangle their most beloved over this issue. The problem with depression, is it is truly unimaginable for those who have not suffered it. Of course, everyone has been sad. Unfortunately, sadness is to depression like Pooh Bear is to a live Grizzly.

Depression is a weight on your chest. A feeling of abandonment, of overwhelming exhaustion, of complete aloneness, of a darkness that will never end. And if you understand this paragraph because you have had or do have these feeling, I am so sorry.

This is the part where the family and friends want to say, "But it will get better," "just stick it out," etc. And I can't, because unfortunately there are no guarantees. But I can tell you that I have seen light in that darkness before, on more than one occasion. And it took a hell of a long time and a lot of work to get there, but it was so worth it. Because it is beautiful. And it is not just amazing for you, it is amazing for everyone you love and who loves you.

Now here is the hard part. Here, is reality. Here, list the people that love you, the people that rely on you, the people that need you.

1. _____
2. _____
3. _____
4. _____
5. _____
6. _____
7. _____
8. _____
9. _____

Look at that list. All of those people, with their platitudes: they want to see you happy. They truly do love you, and if you ignore the rest of what I have said, remember this: your family and friends would do anything for you if they thought it could make you happy. I know that they cannot fix you, and you know they cannot fix you, but they can and do love you, and they will support you while you fight this fight.

And think about the others who rely on you, even if they do not love you. My pets need me to survive. My office needs me to get work done. My enemies need me to bitch about. The store I shop in weekly needs me to help keep it in business. You get the idea. While it may seem like very few, if any, people need you around, you might be surprised by how many lives you impact.

FAMILY & FRIENDS: Hopefully, your depressed loved one knows you want to help. The best help is being there and offering a shoulder when necessary. Sometimes, you may be asked for advice. Sometimes not. It's the being there that matters the most.

Reflection Section:

_____

_____

_____

_____

_____

_____

_____

_____

CHAPTER 5

'Til Death Do You Part

"Suicide is not a remedy." - **James Garfield**

Death is not a joke. Suicide is not a joke. When I was in seventh grade, my language arts teacher had us record a phrase or saying every day, only one of which I remember: suicide is a permanent solution to a temporary problem. I cannot say that I agree with that concept completely, as some problems are a little more permanent than others. But the first part is inarguable; you can never take suicide back. You can never repair the holes in the hearts of the loved ones you leave behind, you can never again pet your dog, or eat an ice cream cone. You can never feel the sunshine again, or hope that someday will be better.

It is so hard to focus on the "S" word. Suicide is the most permanent of all steps. And now, I break my own rule on statistic citing. According to Suicide.Org, as of 2005, 1.3% of deaths each year in the United States were suicides.[i] That equals one (1) death by suicide almost every seventeen minutes.[ii] You do not want to be a statistic. Neither do I. So instead of focusing on suicide, focus on something that is malleable, workable, doable.

Instead, focus on the "C" word. Cope. Make sure that your coping skills outweigh your depressive thoughts. Because ultimately coping skills are any depressed person's closest ally. I love my family and friends, as I am sure you love yours. But coping skills build the wall the keep us safe from the very darkest of paths. Coping skills lift us up, each time depression brings us down.

* If you do feel suicidal, please call someone. If you are not comfortable calling a family member or friend, try one of these resources:

National Suicide Prevention: 1-800-273-8255

National Suicide Hotline: 1-800-SUICIDE

SAFE (Self-Abuse Finally Ends): 800-DONT-CUT

1. Mad Coping Skillz for All You Gangstas' Out There

As cool as that title may sound, I cannot tell you how to cope. I cannot necessarily even teach you how to cope. But, I can tell you my favorite ways to cope. I love to play with my dogs. I love to cuddle up with a book. Or go out to eat by myself, because the funny looks I sometimes get sort of crack me up. Or hear my little brother laugh. Or talk to my dad. Or box— beating the sh*t out of my punching bag makes me feel awesome.

But coping is not always about doing things that bring pleasure. Coping skills are primarily about dealing with the parts of your life that are hard, the parts of your life that are deepening your depression. If you hate your job, you look for a new one. If you are overwhelmed by your family, grab a book, and take a nice bubble bath. Go for a walk. If you are not allergic to exercise like I am, try that. Whatever works for you.

Just try. Please. If not for yourself, for your family or your friends. Try to think of some coping skills that work for you, and write them down, so if the darkness comes back, you have a tangible reminder of where you can turn.

_____

_____

_____

_____

And I know, it sounds so much simpler than it is. But guess what? Just reading this book is a coping skill. You are ACTIVELY doing something because you want to fight off the depression. Or because you want to understand depression better. And every brick of understanding that you lay strengthens your fight against the dark.

FAMILY & FRIENDS: Let's be honest. If your loved one has reached this point, you are probably also at your wit's end. And that is absolutely alright. Because depression impacts everyone it touches, directly or indirectly. Such is the nature of the beast. That being said, every interaction with your loved one does not have to be depression focused. You can (and should) still go to movies, grab a bite to eat, and just be normal. Spending time doing everyday activities is a great way to help your loved one cope. And help you not to get the 'blues,' yourself!

Side Note: 'Cutting' is a coping skill. But it is not a healthy one. When I say find coping skills that work for you, you need to make sure you are finding skills that are healthy. If you have unhealthy skills, find a healthy alternative. Instead of cutting, put a rubber band around your wrist and snap it when you feel the need to cut. If you want to smoke to cope, suck on a hard candy instead. Be smart. Be healthy.

Reflection Section:_____
_____
_____
_____

CHAPTER 6

The End of My Ramblings and the Beginning of Tomorrow

"You can only come to the morning through the shadows."

-J.R.R. Tolkien

I wish I could promise you that your depression will be forever cured some day. I wish someone could make that promise to me. And for many, many depressed individuals, that will be absolutely true. It won't be true for all of us. But we will have good days, good weeks, months, and even years. And as science progresses, new and more effective medicines come out regularly. Trust that you can beat your depression.

Find yourself some professional help. Find yourself some trusted friends and family. Find yourself stepping out of the of depression.

I believe in you. And I know you believe in me. Thanks for your time.

_____

_____

_____

_____

_____

_____

_____

_____

_____

_____

_____

_____

_____

_____

Name the five (5) people you trust the most.

_____

_____

_____

_____

_____

_____

_____

_____

_____

_____

_____

_____

_____

_____

_____

_____

_____

Write about the scariest moment you have experienced.

_____

_____

_____

_____

_____

_____

_____

_____

_____

_____

_____

_____

_____

_____

_____

_____

_____

_____

_____

What is your happiest memory?

_____

_____

_____

_____

_____

_____

_____

_____

_____

_____

_____

_____

_____

_____

_____

_____

_____

_____

_____

Describe your perfect vacation.

_____

_____

_____

_____

_____

_____

_____

_____

_____

_____

_____

_____

_____

_____

_____

_____

_____

Describe your perfect day.

_____

_____

_____

_____

_____

_____

_____

_____

_____

_____

_____

_____

_____

_____

_____

_____

_____

_____

What is your saddest memory?

_____

_____

_____

_____

_____

_____

_____

_____

_____

_____

_____

_____

_____

_____

_____

_____

_____

_____

If you could have any job on earth and money didn't matter, whay job would you choose?

_____

_____

_____

_____

_____

_____

_____

_____

_____

_____

_____

_____

_____

_____

_____

_____

_____

What is the best thing that ever happened to you?

_____

_____

_____

_____

_____

_____

_____

_____

_____

_____

_____

_____

_____

_____

_____

_____

_____

_____

Who is your best friend? Why?

_____

_____

_____

_____

_____

_____

_____

_____

_____

_____

_____

_____

_____

_____

_____

_____

_____

_____

_____

Name five (5) things that you can do to brighten
your mood without spending any money.

_____

_____

_____

_____

_____

_____

_____

_____

_____

_____

_____

_____

_____

_____

_____

_____

_____

_____

What is the hardest thing you have ever experienced?

_____

_____

_____

_____

_____

_____

_____

_____

_____

_____

_____

_____

_____

_____

_____

_____

_____

_____

Name the five (5) people who depend on you the most.

_____

_____

_____

_____

_____

_____

_____

_____

_____

_____

_____

_____

_____

_____

_____

_____

_____

_____

Describe your perfect meal.

_____

_____

_____

_____

_____

_____

_____

_____

_____

_____

_____

_____

_____

_____

_____

_____

_____

_____

What is the funniest joke you know?

_____

_____

_____

_____

_____

_____

_____

_____

_____

_____

_____

_____

_____

_____

_____

_____

_____

_____

Doodle all over this page.

What do you like best about yourself?

_____

_____

_____

_____

_____

_____

_____

_____

_____

_____

_____

_____

_____

_____

_____

_____

_____

_____

Describe your first kiss.

_____

_____

_____

_____

_____

_____

_____

_____

_____

_____

_____

_____

_____

_____

_____

_____

_____

_____

Who is your closest family member? Why?

_____

_____

_____

_____

_____

_____

_____

_____

_____

_____

_____

_____

_____

_____

_____

_____

_____

_____

What is your biggest regret?

_____
_____
_____
_____
_____
_____
_____
_____
_____
_____
_____
_____
_____
_____
_____
_____
_____
_____
_____

Who in your life knows you the best?

_____

_____

_____

_____

_____

_____

_____

_____

_____

_____

_____

_____

_____

_____

_____

_____

_____

_____

Write a letter of apology to someone you wish to apologize to (and no, you don't have to send it).

_____

_____

_____

_____

_____

_____

_____

_____

_____

_____

_____

_____

_____

_____

_____

_____

_____

_____

What would you most like to change about yourself?

_____

_____

_____

_____

_____

_____

_____

_____

_____

_____

_____

_____

_____

_____

_____

_____

_____

_____

What is the funniest thing you have ever experienced?

_____

_____

_____

_____

_____

_____

_____

_____

_____

_____

_____

_____

_____

_____

_____

_____

---

[i] http://www.suicide.org/suicide-statistics.html#2005r
[ii] See id.

Nothing in this book was written by a professional and should not be used as, or in place of, professional advice. This book is solely one depression survivor's thoughts, feelings, and suggestions on the intimidating world of depression. Special thanks to everyone who inadvertently influenced the epic talent of the author.